planet earth

AMAZING ANIMALS OF THE RAINFOREST

By Tracey West

SCHOLASTIC INC.

New York   Toronto   London   Auckland   Sydney
Mexico City   New Delhi   Hong Kong   Buenos Aires

Photo Copyright Credits

Front Cover (foreground): Chris Hill / Shutterstock. Front cover (background): Huw Cordey. Back Cover: BBC Planet Earth / Ben Osborne; Thomas Mangelsen / Minden Pictures.

Page 1: Ferenc Cegledi / Shutterstock, Keel-billed Toucan. Page 3: Steve Winter/National Geographic Image Collection. Pages 4-5 (background): szefei / Shutterstock. Page 4 (insets, top to bottom): Siloto / Shutterstock; Edward Parker / Alamy. Page 5 (insets, top to bottom): Jonny McCullagh / Shutterstock; Paul Souders / Corbis. Pages 6-7 (background): Huw Cordey. Pages 8-9 (background): Huw Cordey. Page 8 (insets, top to bottom): Seapics.com; Thomas Mangelsen / Minden Pictures; Pete Oxford/Minden Pictures. Page 9 (insets, top to bottom): Michael Nichols / National Geographic Image Collection; iamtheking33 / Fotolia. Pages 10-11 (background): Seapics.com, Tucuxi leaping. Page 10-11 (top): National Geographic / Getty Images. Page 10 (top inset): Sea World of California / Corbis. Page 10 (bottom left inset): BBC Planet Earth. Page 10 (bottom right inset): H. Reinhard / Peter Arnold Inc. Page 11 (insets, top to bottom): Flip Nicklin / Minden Pictures; Seapics.com. Pages 12-13 (background): Arco Images GmbH / Alamy. Page 12 (inset): Hippocampus Bildarchiv. Page 13 (top): Blickwinkel / Alamy. Pages 14-15 (background): SA Team / Foto Natura / Minden Pictures. Pages 14-15 (top banner): Laurance B. Aiuppy / Getty Images. Page 15 (insets, top to bottom): Silvestre Silva / FLPA / Photo Researchers, Inc.; Edward Parker / Alamy. Pages 16-17 (background): Tom Brakefield / Getty Images. Page 17 (insets, top to bottom): James Warwick / Getty Images; Thomas Mangelsen / Minden Pictures. Pages 18-19 (background): Michael & Patricia Fogden / Minden Pictures. Page 19 (inset): Blickwinkel / Alamy. Pages 20-21 (background): Gerard Lacz / Peter Arnold Inc. Page 20 (inset): Nicholas Parfitt / Getty Images. Pages 22-23 (background): Gerry Ellis / Minden Pictures. Pages 22-23 (top): VisionsofAmerica / Joe Sohm / Getty Images. Page 22 (insets, top to bottom): Steve Winter / National Geographic Image Collection; Pete Oxford / Minden Pictures. Pages 24-25 (background): Joe McDonald / Corbis. Page 24 (inset): Joe McDonald/Corbis. Page 25 (center inset): Pete Oxford / naturepl.com. Page 25 (right insets, top to bottom): Kevin Schafer / Corbis; Luiz C. Marigo / Peter Arnold Inc. Pages 26-27 (background): Paul Souders / Corbis. Pages 26-27 (top): Jeremy Horner / Getty Images. Page 27 (insets, top to bottom): Mike Birkhead / OSF / Photo Library; Michael Nichols / National Geographic Image Collection. Pages 28-29 (background): Nick Garbutt / naturepl.com. Page 28 (inset): Theo Allofs / Corbis. Page 29 (center inset): Pete Oxford / Minden Pictures. Page 29 (right insets, top to bottom): Luciano Candisani / Minden Pictures; Roy Toft / National Geographic Image Collection. Pages 30-31 (background): M. Watson / ardea.com. Page 30 (inset): M. Watson / ardea.com. Page 31 (center inset): Cyril Ruoso / Minden Pictures. Page 31 (right insets, top to bottom): WILDLIFE / Peter Arnold Inc.; Adrienne Gibson / Animals Animals. Pages 32-33 (background): Michael & Patricia Fogden / Minden Pictures. Page 32 (insets, left to right): Steve Kaufman / CORBIS; Dr. Rudolf G. Arndt / Visuals Unlimited. Page 33 (insets, top to bottom): Flip De Nooyer / Minden Pictures; Ferenc Cegledi / Shutterstock. Pages 34-35 (background): Richard R. Hansen / Photo Researchers, Inc. Page 34 (top inset): Erwin & Peggy Bauer / Animals Animals. Page 34 (bottom left inset): David Haring / OSF / Photo Library. Page 34 (bottom right inset): Rod Williams / naturepl.com. Page 35 (inset): Gail Shumway / Getty Images. Pages 36-37 (background): Heidi & Hans-Juergen Koch / Minden Pictures. Page 37 (insets, top to bottom): Tom Brakefield / DRK Photo; Joe McDonald / DRK Photo, Joe McDonald / DRK Photo. Pages 38-39 (background): Tui De Roy / Minden Pictures. Pages 38-39 (top): National Geographic / Getty Images. Page 39 (insets, top to bottom): Pete Oxford / Minden Pictures; W. Perry Conway / CORBIS; Pages 40-41 (background): Michael Fogden / OSF / Photo Library. Page 40 (insets, top to bottom): Connie Coleman / Getty Images; Dan Wood / istockphoto.com. Page 41 (inset): Barbara Tripp / Shutterstock. Pages 42-43 (background): Gunter Ziesler / Peter Arnold Inc. Page 42 (inset): Bullit Marquez / AP Photo. Page 43 (inset): WILDLIFE / Peter Arnold Inc. Pages 44-45 (background): Tim Laman / National Geographic Image. Page 44 (insets, top to bottom) Phil Savoie / naturepl.com; J & C Sohns/Picture Press/Photo Library. Pages 46-47 (top, left to right): NASA / bdh; Tom Hugh-Jones; DCI / Martin Kilmek / Discovery; BBC Planet Earth / Ben Osborne; NASA / bdh; BBC NHU; DCI / Ed Carreon; Ben Dilley. Pages 46-47 (bottom, left to right): NASA / bdh; Tom Hugh-Jones; Peter Scoones; BBC Planet Earth / Ben Osborne; BBC Planet Earth / Ben Osborne; NASA / bdh; Barrie Britton; BBC Planet Earth. Page 47 (map): Newscom. Page 48 (spot): Page 48 (top, left to right): NASA / bdh; Tom Hugh-Jones; DCI / Martin Kilmek / Discovery; BBC Planet Earth / Ben Osborne. Page 48 (bottom, left to right): NASA / bdh; Tom Hugh-Jones; Peter Scoones; BBC NHU.

ISBN-13: 978-0-545-10917-8

ISBN-10: 0-545-10917-5

BBC (word mark and logo) are trademarks of the British Broadcasting Corporation and are used under license.

Planet Earth logo © BBC 2006. BBC logo © BBC 1996. Love Earth logo TM BBC.

Published by Scholastic Inc.

SCHOLASTIC and associated logos are trademarks and/or registered trademarks of Scholastic Inc.

12 11 10 9 8 7 6 5 4 3 2   9 10 11 12/0

Cover design by Michael Massen. Interior design by Michael Massen and Two Red Shoes design.

Printed in the U.S.A.

Printed on paper containing minimum of 30% post-consumer fiber.

First printing, January 2009

Contents

What Is a Rainforest? 4

Types of Rainforests 6

Rainforest Layers..................... 8

Orange Spot Freshwater Stingray . 10

Red-Bellied Piranha 10

Tucuxi...................... 11

Dorado 12

Spectacled Caiman 13

Agouti.......................14

Sumatran Tiger 16

Bengal Tiger 17

Leaf-Cutter Ants....................18

Goliath Bird-Eating Tarantula 19

African Forest Elephant 20

Sumatran Rhinoceros 21

Ocelot.......................22

Jaguar.......................23

Short-Tailed Leaf-Nosed Bat 24

Rufous-Tailed Jacamar 25

Chimpanzee 26

Proboscis Monkey...................28

Brown Capuchin Monkey.......... 29

Brown Howler Monkey...............30

Long-Tailed Macaque.........................31

Ruby-Throated Hummingbird 32

Masked Tityra....................... 32

Hoatzin............................. 33

Keel-Billed Toucan 33

Tree Anteater 34

Lesser Slow Loris.................. 34

Red-Eyed Tree Frog 35

Green Anaconda 36

Harpy Eagle........................38

Birdwing Butterfly 40

Blue Morpho Butterfly 40

Glasswing Butterfly 41

Tawny Owl Butterfly.................41

Monkey-Eating Eagle 42

Eagle Owl 43

Raggiana Bird of Paradise 44

Blue Bird of Paradise 45

Glossary......................... 46

Tropical Rainforests

of the World.................... 47

Protect Planet Earth 48

What Is a Rainforest?

A rainforest is a tropical forest, usually of tall, densely growing evergreen trees in an area of high annual rainfall. It is home to millions of plants and animals. In a rainforest, you'll find these four things:

Rain:

It rains between 65 and 100 inches a year in a rainforest, more than anywhere else in the world.

Sun:

Many rainforests are located in tropical areas near the equator. Here the sun shines for 12 hours a day, which helps plants grow.

Plants:

Rainforests only cover 3 percent of the Earth's surface, but are home to one-half of the world's plants. A typical rainforest is filled with trees, vines, and flowers that grow so closely together that if you're on the rainforest floor, the canopy of the trees hides the sky above.

Animals:

Scientists estimate that more than half of all the world's animals live in rainforests. There are countless species of fish that live in the rivers that act as arteries of any rainforest.

Types of Rainforests

Lowland Tropical Forest:

These are the largest areas of rainforest in the world. Clustered close to the equator, they contain millions of plants that grow very close together. In these forests, the trees stay green all year round.

Tropical Deciduous Forest:

These forests are located in tropical areas of the world, such as Jalisco, Mexico, but they're a little farther away from the equator than the lowland forests. There is usually a dry period for a few months, causing some of the trees to shed their leaves.

Flooded Forest:

In some parts of the world, rivers near rainforests flood once a year. This happens in the Amazon basin, when the Amazon river floods its banks. For about half the year, the rainforest floor is submerged, and the habitat changes. New sources of food are available, and new migration patterns develop as a result.

Tropical Mountain Forest:

Also called a cloud forest, these rainforests grow on high mountaintops throughout the world. The temperature is cooler here than in lowland rainforests, but they are still very wet places. The humidity is often at 100%, and the moisture from the fog and clouds allows epiphytes—like orchids, mosses, and other plants that attach themselves to other plants—to flourish.

Mangrove Forest:

These special forests can be found where the land meets the sea, such as in areas of South Florida, or Southeast Asia. Mangrove trees grow in the water and the roots of the trees grow up out of the mud so they can absorb oxygen. These unique environments provide a safe nursery ground for fish, and support a wide variety of birds, reptiles, and shellfish.

Rainforest Layers

A rainforest can be divided into different layers, each one home to different kinds of animals and plants. The animals in this scrapbook are grouped together according to the layers they live in.

Water:

This is the bottom layer of a Flooded Forest or Mangrove Forest. Many river-dwelling animals, such as freshwater dolphins, migrate to these forests when the rivers flood.

Forest Floor:

This is the bottom layer of a typical rainforest. The trees here grow very tall, so as to compete for as much sunlight as possible. This is why very little sunlight reaches this layer (approximately 2%). The forest floor is home to lots of insects as well as large, land-dwelling animals such as gorillas and elephants.

Understory:

This is the area above the ground but underneath the leaves of the trees. Like the forest floor, the understory is cool and dark. Jaguars and leopards live in branches of the trees here.

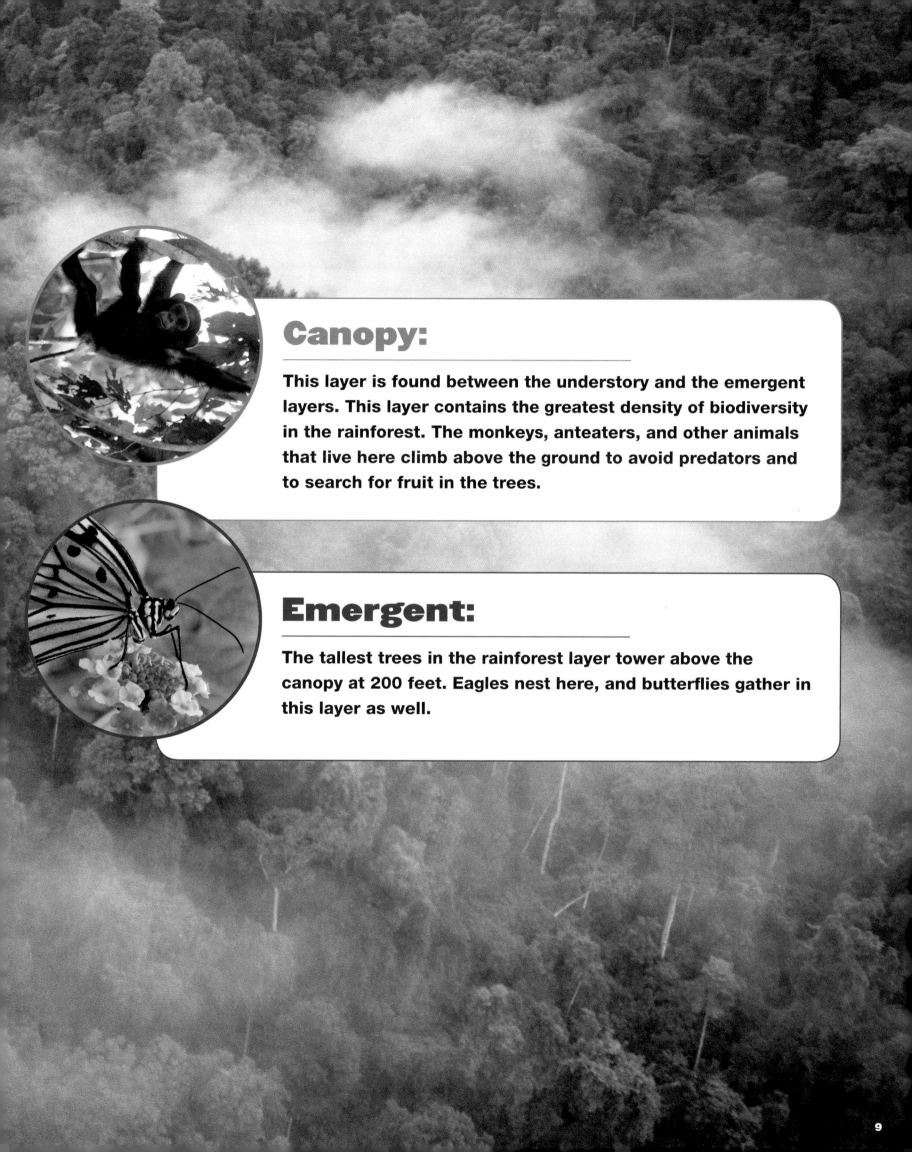

Canopy:

This layer is found between the understory and the emergent layers. This layer contains the greatest density of biodiversity in the rainforest. The monkeys, anteaters, and other animals that live here climb above the ground to avoid predators and to search for fruit in the trees.

Emergent:

The tallest trees in the rainforest layer tower above the canopy at 200 feet. Eagles nest here, and butterflies gather in this layer as well.

ORANGE SPOT FRESHWATER STINGRAY

ANATOMY 101

- Gills on top of the head let the stingray breathe while it is partially buried in sand or mud.
- Having a mouth on your belly might seem weird to you, but it's useful for the stingray. It can move its body over prey, and then suck it up!
- This fish can get as big as 3 feet long from head to tail.
- This tail isn't just sharp—it's venomous! The stingray mostly uses its stinger to defend itself.

FISH

Species: *Potamortrygon motoro*

Also known as: South American freshwater stingray

Average weight: 8 to 10 pounds

Average size: 18 inches in diameter; as long as 3 feet from head to tail

Where it lives: The Amazon River

Watch that stinger! **This relative of a** shark **doesn't have teeth, but its sharp tail is a** painful weapon.

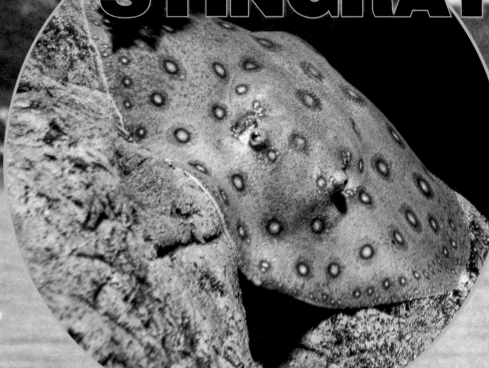

A piranha's teeth are shaped like triangles that fit together like the blades of a scissor.

This rainforest species has the *sharpest* teeth and most powerful jaws of any piranha.

School's In

These piranhas travel together in large schools, mainly eating small fish and fruit, but if they come across a large animal that's sick or vulnerable, they can quickly tear it apart with their long teeth.

RED-BELLIED PIRANHA

FISH

Species: *Pygocentrus nattereri*

Maximum weight: Up to 8 pounds

Maximum length: 12 to 24 inches

Where it lives: Rivers in South America

Favorite meal: Other fish, insects

TUCUXI

When a rainforest **floods,** this freshwater *"river dolphin"* migrates into the area to *search for food.*

The tucuxi (pronounced: too-koo-shee) looks a lot like a bottlenose dolphin, but it's much smaller—usually about four feet long.

MAMMAL

Species: *Sotallia fluviatillis*

Also known as: River dolphin

Average weight: About 100 pounds

Average length: 4 to 5 feet

Where it lives: Rivers, bays, and lakes in South America

Favorite meal: Fish

People *fish* for this animal in the **rivers** of *South America*.

DORADO

In Argentina, this fish is known as the "tiger of the Paraná," a river that runs through the country. This fish is called this because it fights back when it is caught on a hook by fishermen.

FISH

Species: *Salminus maxillosus*

Average weight: More than 40 pounds

Average length: 39 inches

Where it lives: Rivers in northern Argentina, Brazil, and Bolivia

ANATOMY 101

- Dorado means "golden" in Spanish. This fish gets its name from its striking yellow, orange, and black scales.

- The largest dorado ever caught weighed 75 pounds.

- This carnivorous fish has sharp teeth that help it chow down on smaller fish.

SPECTACLED CAIMAN

This member of the *alligator* family spends **most** of its life in **water**.

Family Ties

Female spectacled caimans lay their eggs in nests they build on the ground. When the babies hatch, they form groups, and remain together until they're about a year and a half old.

REPTILE

Species: *Caiman crocodilus*

Also known as: Common caiman, tinga

Average length: 3 to 6 feet

Where it lives: Rivers, wetlands, and rainforests in Central and South America

ANATOMY 101

• A bony ridge around the caiman's eyes make people think of eyeglasses, or "spectacles"—that's how it received its name.

• A long, muscular tail propels the spectacled caiman through the water.

• Its webbed feet help the caiman swim.

• Most caimans measure up to 7 or 8 feet long—but some can grow up to 10 feet.

AGOUTI

These *rodents* play a role
in keeping the *rainforest* alive.

MAMMAL

Species: *Dasyprocta punctata*

Average weight: 2 to 9 pounds

Average length: 16 to 25 inches

Where it lives: Central and
South America, east of the
Andes Mountains

ANATOMY 101

• This nimble rodent can grow up to 2 feet long and weigh up to 9 pounds.

• The agouti can crack open hard Brazil nutshells with its sharp teeth.

• An agouti's tail is only about an inch long.

Nut Crackers

Brazil nut trees tower over rainforests in South America. Brazil nuts grow inside hard pods that look like coconuts. Agoutis not only eat Brazil nuts, but they help the trees to grow, too. How? They bury extra nuts in the ground to eat later, and the nuts they forget to retrieve sometimes grow into Brazil nut trees.

When danger is near, an agouti will grunt, squeal, and bark to warn others.

Indonesia used to be home to three kinds of tigers: the Bali tiger, the Java tiger, and the Sumatran tiger. Now, both the Bali and the Java tigers have become extinct, and Sumatran tigers are critically endangered.

MAMMAL

Species: *Tigris sumatrae*

Average weight: 265 pounds (males), 200 pounds (females)

Average length: 8 feet (males), 7 feet (females)

Where it lives: Only in Sumatra, an island in Indonesia

Favorite meal: Wild pigs, deer, fish, crocodiles, birds

ANATOMY 101

- Webbing between the toes makes these cats fast swimmers.

- White spots on the back of the tiger's ears are called "eye spots" or "predator spots." They may be used to fool predators attempting to sneak up on the tiger from behind—as these spots can be mistaken for eyes.

- Long whiskers act as sensors to help these tigers move through the thick vegetation on the rainforest floor.

- At night, a Sumatran tiger can see six times better than a human.

- Its dark red coat and closely spaced black stripes camouflage the tiger in the forest.

SUMATRAN TIGER

Fewer than 500 of these tigers inhabit the rainforests of the *Indonesian island* of Sumatra.

BENGAL TIGER

These *tigers* can be found **roaming** the *mangrove forests* of India and **Bangladesh.**

Night Hunters

Bengal tigers hunt at night. Their favorite meals are deer, wild boar, and monkeys. To hunt their prey, they use a stalk and ambush approach. The tigers silently follow their prey and when they are close, they run in to make the kill.

Bengal tigers can eat up to 65 pounds of meat a night.

MAMMAL

Species: *Panthera tigris*

Average weight: 500 pounds (male), 300 pounds (female)

Average length: 10 feet (male), 9 feet (female)

Where it lives: The mangrove forests of India and Bangladesh

Favorite meal: Wild ox and buffalo

These ants turn *leaves* into a special fungus they can *eat*.

Fungus Farmers

Leaf-cutter ants live in underground colonies of 3 to 8 million ants! Each ant has a special job.

Foragers: These ants march for miles in search of leaves. They use their sharp jaws to cut the leaves and then bring them back to the colony.

Gardeners: Ants can't digest leaves, so the gardener ants use the leaves to make fungus that they can digest. First, they lick the leaves clean; then they grind them up; and finally they deposit dung on them. Then fungus grows on the dung. Yummy!

Defenders: These soldier ants protect the colony from attack by other ants.

INSECT

Species: *Atta cephalotes*

Average length: About 0.5 inch

Where it lives: Tropical rainforests and other forests in parts of Central America, South America, and North America

LEAF-CUTTER ANTS

GOLIATH BIRD-EATING TARANTULA

When the rainforest floods, the goliath will climb into the trees to stay dry.

Despite its name, this **huge spider** mostly dines on *bugs*, rodents, and **frogs**.

ANATOMY 101

- This spider spans 12 inches wide from leg to leg. That's about the size of a small pizza!
- The tarantula has sharp, tiny hairs on its legs that can be shot at enemies.
- The goliath kills prey with a venomous bite, but don't worry—this poison isn't strong enough to kill humans.

INSECT

Species: *Theraposa blondi*

Average weight of adult male: About 4 ounces

Average length of adult male: About 11 inches

Where it lives: Rainforests on the coast of northeastern South America

MAMMAL

Species: *Loxodonta cyclotis*

Average weight: 3,690 to 7,040 pounds

Average height: About 8 feet

Where it lives: Forests near the equator in Africa

ANATOMY 101

- Their straight tusks are less likely to get caught in the underbrush than the curved tusks of other elephant species.

- When these elephants get hot, they can flap their big ears to fan themselves. Their ears are packed with blood vessels to help them disperse heat quickly and keep them cool.

- They are able to walk quietly through the forest thanks to their wide, padded feet.

- They use their long trunks to do many things: breathe, smell, spray water, uproot trees, pick up food, and— of course!—make noise.

AFRICAN FOREST ELEPHANT

These **elephants** live in forests near the equator in *Central Africa.*

SUMATRAN RHINOCEROS

It might have two *sharp horns*, but this **massive** mammal is a *peaceful* plant eater.

During the hottest hours of the day, Sumatran rhinos wallow in muddy water to beat the heat.

MAMMAL

Species: *Dicerorhinus sumatrensis*

Also known as: Asian two-horned rhinoceros

Average weight: 0.8 ton

Average length: 8 to 10.5 feet, plus a 20-inch tail

Where it lives: Tropical rainforests in Indonesia

Rhinos in Danger

There are fewer than 400 Sumatran rhinos left in the world today. They've lost habitat from large areas of rainforest that have been cut down.

MAMMAL

Species: *Felis pardalis*

Average weight of adult male: 24 to 35 pounds

Average length of adult male: 28 to 35 inches (not including tail)

Where it lives: from Texas south to Argentina

Solitary Hunters

Ocelots usually live alone. They like to hunt at night for prey such as rabbits, rodents, iguanas, frogs, and small turtles. Even though they are great tree climbers, they prefer to hunt on the ground.

This *nocturnal cat* stays hidden in the rainforest **underbrush** during the *day*.

ANATOMY 101

- The ocelot's coat is considered to be the most beautiful fur of any big cat. This is bad news for the ocelot, which has been hunted for its fur.

- The average adult ocelot is about 28 to 35 inches long, not including the tail, and weighs 24 to 35 pounds.

OCELOT

JAGUAR

This strong, *silent* cat is a symbol of power in Central and *South America*.

Keeping Cool

Life in a rainforest can get hot and steamy. A jaguar cools off by swimming or hanging out in a stream. The jaguar and tiger are the only two big cats in the world that are good swimmers. While in the water, the jaguar sometimes catches fish to eat.

A Hunter's Habitat

The thick vegetation of a rainforest is an ideal hunting ground for a jaguar. The jaguar can hide near the rainforest border and wait for prey to pass by. When it makes a kill, it usually drags it deep into the forest, where it can feed without being disturbed.

MAMMAL

Species: *Panthera onca*

Also known as: El tigre or tigre Americano

Average weight of adult male: 220 to 350 pounds

Average length of adult male: 5.6 feet to 9 feet, including tail

Where it lives: Mexico and Central and South America

Favorite meal: Just about whatever it can catch, including capybaras, deer, armadillos, and monkeys

23

SHORT-TAILED LEAF-NOSED BAT

These **nighttime** flyers help bring destroyed areas of *rainforest* back to **life.**

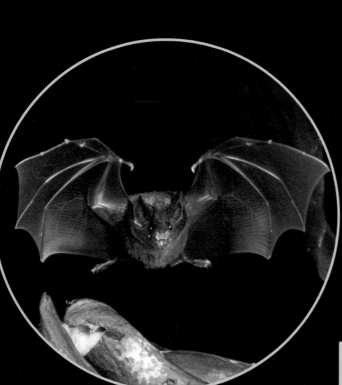

D id You Know?
About one out of every
500 of these bats is
bright orange!

MAMMAL

Species: *Carollia perspecillata*

Also known as: Short-tailed fruit bat

Average weight: 0.6 of an ounce

Average length: 1.9 to 2.6 inches

Where it lives: Mexico, Bolivia, Paraguay, Brazil, and the Caribbean Islands

Seed Spreaders

When the sun goes down, short-tailed leaf-nosed bats go to work. The bats fly through the understory looking for fruit to eat. When they find some, they find a safe perch and eat it, seeds and all. When they're done eating, they take a short nap before repeating this cycle again and again — all night long!

As the bat flies through the understory, it carries pollen on its body, pollinating the flowers as it goes. It also poops out the seeds it hasn't digested. These seeds fall to the ground, and new plants grow. A single bat can "plant" as many as 60,000 seeds in one night.

ANATOMY 101

- Jacamars are known for the glittery green feathers on their upper body and upper breast.
- The long, slender bill is sometimes called a "needle beak."

BIRD

Species: *Galbula ruficauda*

Average weight: About 1 ounce

Average length: 9 inches with a 2-inch-long bill

Where it lives: Mexico, Ecuador, Bolivia, Argentina, Colombia, Venezuela, the Guianas, Brazil, and Trinidad and Tobago

Butterflies for Breakfast

You may think a butterfly is beautiful to look at, but when a jacamar sees a butterfly, it sees a meal. When a butterfly flies by, the jacamar chases it, catching it with its beak. Then, the jacamar goes back to its perch, and pounds the butterfly against a branch before gobbling it down.

These colorful *birds* perch on low **shrubs** in the **understory** of the rainforest and hunt for *butterflies* and **dragonflies.**

RUFOUS-TAILED JACAMAR

Grooming is important to chimps. They often spend hours picking bugs and twigs out of each other's fur.

These apes eat, sleep, and *play* in the trees of the *rainforest* canopy.

CHIMPANZEE

Hey You!

Chimps have many ways to communicate with each other. They grunt, bark, and make gestures with their hands. They also make a loud noise called a pant-hoot. Each chimp has its own pant-hoot so that the other chimps know which one of them is calling out. A pant-hoot might be used to let other chimps know danger is near, or if food has been found.

They're a Lot Like Us!

Chimpanzees are the closest living relatives to humans. We share more than 98% of the same DNA. Here are some other ways chimps and humans are alike:

• We both live in communities: Chimps live in social groups that contain several dozen members.

• We both use tools: When they need to gather food or water, chimps use sticks, stones, and leaves to help them. They also use sticks as weapons, throwing them at their enemies.

• We're both omnivores: Chimps mostly eat fruits, nuts, and plants, but they also eat insects and eggs, and they sometimes hunt for medium-sized animals.

MAMMAL

Species: *Pan troglodyte*

Average weight: 90 to 120 pounds (male), 60 to 110 pounds (female)

Average height: 4 feet

Where it lives: Tropical rainforests, bamboo forests, swamps, and other areas of Africa

These *long-nosed* monkeys like to **live** near *water*, away from human **settlements**.

Proboscis monkeys have webbing between their fingers that helps them swim. These monkeys can swim underwater, and they're high divers, too! They can leap into the water from the upper branches of trees.

Old vs. New

Monkeys can be divided into two groups: Old World and New World. Old World monkeys, such as the proboscis, have thick tails that help them balance. New World monkeys, such as the capuchin, have tails that they can use to grab things (called prehensile tails).

ANATOMY 101

- The word *proboscis* means "prominent nose."
- This belly may look fat, but it actually holds a large stomach with many chambers. The proboscis monkey eats a special diet of starchy fruits, leaves, and seeds. The food sits around in its belly and ferments for a while before the monkey can digest it.

PROBOSCIS MONKEY

MAMMAL

Species: *Nasalis larvatus*

Average weight: 35 to 48 pounds (males), 15 to 26 pounds (females)

Average length: 27 inches (males), 24 inches (females)

Where it lives: In mangrove forests and some rainforests in Borneo, an island in Southeast Asia

BROWN CAPUCHIN MONKEY

Brown capuchins are thought to be more intelligent than any other monkey.

These **clever** creatures live in the **rainforests** of *South America.*

MAMMAL

Species: *Cebus apella*

Average weight: About 3 to 11 pounds

Average length: 38 inches, including tail

Where it lives: Forests east of the Andes Mountains in South America

Gets Eaten By: Snakes, jaguars, and birds of prey

ANATOMY 101

- Their prehensile tails are like an extra hand or foot; they help the monkeys climb trees in the canopy.
- The brown capuchin has a big jaw so it can eat big pieces of fruit.

It's Good to Be the Leader

Brown capuchins live in small groups of 8 to 15 monkeys. Each group is led by a dominant male. This male leader has a big job. He leads the attack if his group is threatened by predators or other monkeys. On the other hand, the job has its perks: If there is not enough food to go around, the leader gets to eat first.

Tag-a-Longs

Squirrel monkeys like to hang out around brown capuchin monkeys. Why? They follow the capuchins to new food sources. This saves them the job of foraging for food themselves.

BROWN HOWLER MONKEY

What's that sound? It might be this monkey's *incredible* call.

Hooooooowl!

The howler monkey's amazing howl can be heard from more than a mile away! A bone in the monkey's neck vibrates, amplifying the sound. Scientists think they howl as a way to mark their territory.

ANATOMY 101

- Even though they're called brown howler monkeys, this monkey's fur can have shades of red, yellow, and orange.
- A prehensile tail allows howlers to hang from trees when they feed.

MAMMAL

Species: *Alouatta guariba*

Average weight: 11 to 17.6 pounds (males), 8.8 to 11 pounds (females)

Average length: About 22 inches plus a 23-inch tail (males), about 18.5 inches plus 21.5-inch tail (females)

Where it lives: Coastal rainforests in Brazil

During the hottest part of the day, brown howler monkeys take a siesta!

Treetop Dwellers

Brown howlers spend most of their time in trees where they eat leaves, flowers, and fruits.

MAMMAL

Species: *Macaca fascicularis*

Average weight: About 14 pounds (male), about 9 pounds (female)

Average length: About 1.8 feet (male), about 1.5 feet (female)

Where it lives: The islands of Southeast Asia and some countries in Asia

Favorite foods: Fruit, crabs, insects, mushrooms, frogs, octopus, shrimp

Seafood Lovers

When these monkeys search for food in mangrove forests, they will scoop up crabs, frogs, shrimp, and octopi.

ANATOMY 101

- A special pouch inside their cheek stores food so the macaque can eat it later.

Water Escape

Long-tailed macaques are good swimmers. They like to live in trees that hang over rivers. If a predator attacks, they jump off the tree into the water and swim to safety.

LONG-TAILED MACAQUE

These *water-loving* monkeys like to **chow down** on seafood.

RUBY-THROATED HUMMINGBIRD

Fast Flappers

A ruby-throated hummingbird can flap its wings 53 times in just one second! The fast beating of the wings is what makes the "humming" sound hummingbirds are known for.

BIRD

Species: *Archilocus colubris*

Average weight: .07 to .21 ounces

Average length: 3 to 4 inches

Where it lives: North America and Central America

Gets eaten by: Other birds such as loggerhead shrikes, hawks, and blue jays; domestic cats

In *warm* months, you can see this **tropical bird** in parts of *North America*.

ANATOMY 101
• This bird gets its name from the red throat found on males.

These hummingbirds like to eat nectar from flowers—especially red ones.

These common *birds* can be seen **perching** on **branches** in the *canopy*.

MASKED TITYRA

BIRD

Species: *Tityra semifasciata*

Average weight: About 3.1 ounces

Average length: About 8 inches

Where it lives: In tropical forests from Mexico down to Bolivia and Brazil

ANATOMY 101
• The red coloring around this bird's eyes and base of the beak forms a colorful "mask."

HOATZIN

This *rainforest* dweller looks like a **punk-rock** chicken!

ANATOMY 101

• The hoatzin has bacteria in its gut that slowly breaks down the leaves it eats. This bacteria gives off a really bad smell, which is why it's sometimes called "stinkbird."

BIRD

Species: *Opisthocomus hoazin*

Average weight of adult male: 1.8 pounds

Average length of adult male: 24 to 26 inches

Where it lives: In swamps, mangrove forests, lowland flooded forests, and other places in South America

Favorite foods: The leaves and shoots of plants that grow in swamps and marshes

With its *brightly colored* beak, this bird stands out in the **rainforests** of Central and *South America.*

BIRD

Species: *Ramphastos sulfuratus*

Also known as: Bill bird

Average weight: About 14 ounces

Average length: About 26 inches, including its long beak

Where it lives: In Central and South America, from southern Mexico to northern Colombia

Favorite foods: Fruit, insects, lizards, snakes

ANATOMY 101

• The large, colorful bill is what this bird is best known for. Scientists aren't exactly sure why this bill is so big. It's useful for picking and eating fruit, and it may be used as a defensive weapon.

Toucans aren't great flyers, so they hop along from tree to tree.

KEEL-BILLED TOUCAN

Hole Sweet Home

Toucans live in holes in tree trunks. Sometimes they inhabit holes that were made and abandoned by woodpeckers. Oftentimes, a number of toucans will try to fit into one hole. To do that, each toucan will fold its tail over its head to make room for the others.

TREE ANTEATER

A tree anteater can eat 9,000 ants in one day!

ANATOMY 101

- A prehensile tail helps the tree anteater climb trees.
- Tree anteaters have coarse hairs all over their body. This keeps the ants from biting them.
- Inside their long snout is a 16-inch-long tongue with little barbs on it. It's the perfect tool for scooping ants out of an anthill.

MAMMAL

Species: *Tamandua tetradactyla (southern); Tamandua mexicana (northern)*

Also known as: Tamandua

Average weight: 90 to 120 pounds (male), 60 to 110 pounds (female)

Average length: 1.8 to 2.9 feet, plus a tail that's about 1.5 feet long

Where it lives: Tropical rainforests, savannas, and other areas ranging from Mexico down to South America

Like some *birds,* these mammals nest in **tree** trunks.

ANATOMY 101

- Powerful muscles in their hands and feet allow these animals to hang from tree branches.

These *big-eyed* mammals **seldom** leave the *rain- forest* canopy.

LESSER SLOW LORIS

MAMMAL

Species: *Nycticebus pygmaeus*

Average weight: 2 pounds

Average length: 6 to 10 inches

Where it lives: Rainforests in southeast Asian countries and islands, including Thailand, Vietnam, and China

Favorite foods: Large mollusks, birds, small mammals, fruit, lizards, eggs, and insects such as caterpillars and beetles

RED-EYED TREE FROG

It's not hard to *guess* how this canopy dweller got its name!

This snake's jawbones are attached by stretchy ligaments—kind of like rubber bands. This allows the jaw to stretch open wide enough to swallow prey whole!

How It Kills

In water, the anaconda grabs its prey with its jaws and then coils its long body around its prey until it suffocates it. On land, it hangs in trees, drops down on its prey from above, coils around the animal, and squeezes it to death.

GREEN
ANACONDA

This *green giant* will attack and **eat** just about anything it can get its *jaws* around.

ANATOMY 101

- The green anaconda likes to eat animals that live in water. Its eyes and nostrils are on top of its head, which allows it to breathe, watch, and wait for prey while its body is hidden underwater.

- Pythons can grow longer than green anacondas, but anacondas weigh much more—usually around 300 pounds! That's how they've earned the title of largest snake in the world.

- On average, Anacondas can grow to 20 feet long, but some can get as long as 29 feet!

REPTILE

Species: *Eunectes murinus*

Average weight: 330 pounds

Average length: About 20 feet

Where it lives: Tropical rainforests, swamps, marshes, and streams in South America

HARPY EAGLE

Few **people** have seen this *beautiful* bird of *prey* in the **wild.**

Nests in the Sky

Harpy eagles build their nests at the very top of tall Kapok trees, as high as 140 feet above ground. The nests are built from sticks and branches and lined with green plants and animal fur. Each nest is about 5 feet wide.

BIRD

Species: *Harpia harpyja*

Average weight: 8.5 to 12 pounds (male), 14 to 20 pounds (female)

Average wingspan: Up to 7 feet

Average length of body: 35 to 41 inches

Where it lives: Rainforests in Central and South America, from Mexico to northern Argentina

How It Hunts

Even though the harpy eagles' nests are in the emergent layer of the rainforest, they save energy by hunting in the canopy. First, they perch and wait for prey to appear and then they dive after the prey. Smaller prey, such as iguanas, are brought up to the treetops to be eaten. A harpy eagle can only carry about half of its weight, so the heavier prey is taken to a stump or lower branch to be eaten until the remainder of the carcass is light enough to carry.

ANATOMY 101

• The harpy eagle can grow up to 41 inches long with a wingspan of 6.5 feet!

• To catch their food, harpy eagles swoop down and grab their prey with their large hind talons, which are about 5 inches long.

BIRDWING BUTTERFLY

INSECT

Species: *Ornithoptera priamus*

Also known as: Cairns birdwing

Average wingspan: About 7 inches. The female's wingspan can reach nearly 8 inches.

Where it lives: Australia

Favorite food: Flower nectar

ANATOMY 101

- Like all butterflies, the birdwing sips nectar from flowers with its long, tubelike mouth.

Warning Spikes

The caterpillars of this butterfly eat the leaves of poisonous vines in the rainforest. Orange-red spines on their back warn birds that these caterpillars are a deadly meal!

This is the *largest* species of **butterfly** *found* in Australia.

The amazing *coloration* of this creature helps to **protect** it from *predators*.

In a "Flash"

When the blue morpho flaps its wings, the bright blue contrasts with the dull brown color, a phenomenon called "flashing." It makes it look like the butterfly is appearing and disappearing in the air. That's confusing to predators—and good for the blue morpho!

ANATOMY 101

- The top of this butterfly's wings aren't actually colored blue. The scales contain ridges that reflect blue light.
- The color underneath the wing is dull brown mixed with grays, blacks, and reds. When the butterfly sleeps at night it folds up its wings and blends into the foliage around it.

BLUE MORPHO BUTTERFLY

Species: *Morpho menelaus*

Average wingspan: About 6 inches

Where it lives: Tropical rainforests from Mexico to Colombia

Favorite food: The juices of rotting fruit

GLASSWING BUTTERFLY

This unusual *butterfly* has see-through **wings!**

ANATOMY 101

- The see-through scales on the butterfly's wings help it to hide from predators. It can blend in perfectly with whatever's around itself!

INSECT

Species: *Greta oto*

Average wingspan: 2.2 to 2.3 inches

Where it lives: Central America

Some species of glasswing butterflies drink nectar from poisonous plants. This doesn't hurt the butterflies—but it does keep predators from eating them!

TAWNY OWL BUTTERFLY

These large *butterflies* can be easy to **spot** in the **rainforests** of *Central and South America.*

ANATOMY 101

- On the underside of each wing is a large yellow spot that looks like an owl's eye. Some scientists believe when predators see the spots, they think the butterfly is a type of poisonous tree frog and therefore choose to leave it alone.

INSECT

Species: *Caligo memnon*

Average wingspan: 6 to 8 inches

Where it lives: In Central and South America, from Mexico down to the Amazon basin

MONKEY-EATING EAGLE

Although it's called a monkey-eating eagle, flying lemurs are its favorite meal.

This *eagle*, the second-largest in the **world,** is also called the *Philippine Eagle.*

BIRD

Species: *Pithecophaga jefferyi*

Also known as: Philippine eagle

Average weight: About 17 pounds

Average wingspan: About 6.5 feet

Average length of body: 2.4 to 3.3 feet

Where it lives: Islands in the Philippines

Endangered

The monkey-eating eagle is only found in the Philippines and is the national bird of this country. These birds are becoming increasingly endangered because of losing most of their habitat to logging. There are fewer than 400 left in the wild today.

EAGLE OWL

This eagle owl *hunts* for prey in the rainforests of southeast *Asia*.

ANATOMY 101

- During the day, this owl stays concealed among the foliage of trees. But at night, it emerges, using its excellent night vision to hunt.

ANATOMY 101

- A shorter wingspan than other kinds of eagles helps this monkey-eating eagle maneuver through rainforest trees.

BIRD

Species: *Bubo nipalensis*

Also known as: Forest eagle owl, spot-bellied eagle owl

Where it lives: Southeast Asia

Dancing with the Birds

In some species of birds of paradise, the male will break out dance moves to attract a mate. The raggiana bird of paradise begins with some basic moves: hopping around from leg to leg, flapping its wings, and shaking its orange tail feathers. His show peaks when he hops onto a tree branch to puff out the feathers on his "cape" to show off.

BIRD

Species: *Paradisaea raggiana*

Average length of body: 13 to 14 inches

Where it lives: Eastern New Guinea

ANATOMY 101

- People in Papua New Guinea use these birds' plumes (or feathers) to decorate their ceremonial costumes.

- The yellow-striped feathers on the male's neck are shaped like a fan or cape.

These birds dine on flowers that grow in the rainforest treetops.

RAGGIANA
BIRD OF PARADISE

BLUE BIRD OF PARADISE

This *beautiful bird* lives in a small area of **Papua New Guinea**.

There are more than 30 species of birds of paradise in rainforests in Indonesia, Papua New Guinea, and Australia.

Legendary Birds

The feathers of these birds were brought to Spain in 1522 by explorers and given to the king as a gift. The people of Spain thought the feathers were too beautiful to come from birds who lived in forests. They had to be from paradise! That's how these birds got their name.

BIRD

Species: *Paradisaea rudolphi*

Average length of body: About 12 inches

Where it lives: Southeastern New Guinea

Glossary

amphibian: a cold-blooded animal with a backbone that spends part of its life in water, and part on land

canopy: a tall layer of trees in the rainforest that acts as a roof over the lower layers

carnivorous: a living thing that feeds on animals

emergent layer: the top layer of a rainforest

foliage: the leaves of plants or trees

forage: to search for food

habitat: the place where an animal or plant lives

mammal: a warm-blooded animal with a backbone that feeds milk to its young and usually has hair on its skin

predator: an animal that hunts other animals for food

prehensile: a kind of tail that can grab things, the way a hand can

prey: an animal hunted for food

rainforest: a warm, wet forest that is home to millions of plants and animals and gets more than 70 inches of rainfall a year, on average

reptile: a cold-blooded animal with a backbone that lives on land

territory: an area of land that a group of animals or people claim as their home

understory: a layer of plants and small trees that grow underneath the rainforest canopy

Forests of the World

The *green* areas on this map indicate where the world's great forests—including tropical *rainforests*—are located.

World's last remaining great forests

Around 80% of the world's forests have been destroyed since ancient times, half during the past 30 years; deforestation causes an estimated 20% of greenhouse gas emissions.

North America 4,040 sq. mi. (6,500 sq. km) arc of boreal forest (taiga); stores significant amounts of world's CO_2

Russia World's largest boreal forest (taiga), 1.5 million sq. mi. (3.9 million sq. km)

Central America 89,000 sq. mi. (231,000 sq. km.), (around 20% of original forests), migration corridor for birds

Gola Forest 290 sq. mi. (750 sq. km.), home to 250 bird species

Amazon World's largest rainforest, 1.5 million sq. mi. (3.9 million sq. km); 20% of world's oxygen is produced here, half of Earth's species live here

Congo World's second largest rainforest, home to several types of large mammals

South America World's largest single block of remaining temperate rainforests; more rare than tropical rainforests

Southeast Asia World's oldest rainforest, home to hundreds of species at risk of extinction

© 2007 MCT

Source: globalforestwatch.org, Guardian
Graphic: Zitha Olsen, Majbrit Hoyrup

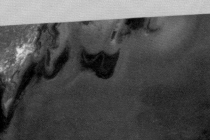

PROTECT PLANET EARTH,
It's the Only One We've Got . . .

Here are some ways you can help.

1. Learn All You Can! Read books and visit websites to learn about what's happening in the rainforest. (www.loveearth.com)

2. Spread the Word. The next time you have to do a book report or project in school, pick one with a rainforest theme. Make a poster, write a song, or read a story about the rainforest.

3. Use Less Paper. Trees are used to make paper. Try to reduce the amount you use. Save paper that has only been used on one side, and use the back for scrap paper.

4. Create an Art Gallery. With your friends or classmates, create paintings or clay sculptures of rainforest animals. Make signs with facts about each animal. Ask if you can post your art gallery in a school or other public place to raise awareness.

5. Shop Smart. Ask your parents to shop for products that weren't made by hurting the rainforest. Look online for responsible ways to buy products like coffee, bananas, and wood.